BEYOND THE MOUNTAINS

BEYOND THE MOUNTAINS

Discovering Blessings in a Cancer Diagnosis

BRUCE KLEIN

Geminae LLC

Editing: Vanessa Vlahaskis

Copyright © 2024 by Bruce Klein

All rights reserved. No part of this book may be reproduced in any manner whatsoever without written permission except in the case of brief quotations embodied in critical articles and reviews.

First Printing, 2024

To Tammy, We began our treatment journeys together on opposite sides of the country. I had hoped we would finish them together and we would have great stories to talk about for years.

To Phil, You were a warrior to the end. Thanks for showing what true courage is.

I hope your new journeys are beautiful and magical.

Contents

Preface   xi
Introduction   xiii

1	How Did This Journey Begin?	1
2	My First Post	7
3	The First Step is Tomorrow	9
4	Waiting is the Hardest Part	11
5	A Metaphysical Post	13
6	Feeling Gratitude	15
7	More Gratitude	17
8	First Cocktail – It's a "TrustFall"	19
9	I am Sooo Tired!	21
10	Learning to Listen to My Body (and Others' Experiences)	23
11	Boston	27
12	The Sun Comes Out	29
13	Just Get Up	31

14	Feeling Good	35
15	Infusion Day #2 – Music	37
16	100 Miles! (We Did It!)	39
17	Oh Well!	41
18	Changing Focus	43
19	Expressing Gratitude	45
20	Infusion Day #3 – Making Adjustments	47
21	Caution: Another Metaphor Coming	49
22	Infusion Day #4	51
23	Hibernation	53
24	Pre-Sleep Vision	59
25	Infusion Day #5	61
26	Side Effects	63
27	Does It Really Suck?	67
28	Yes, This is it! This is One Thing I Have Learned	69
29	I am Slowly Dying	71
30	Honoring My Body	75
31	Vulnerability	79
32	Infusion Day #6 – What a Lucky Day!	81
33	"If/When" Will Never Make Me Happy	83
34	The Duality of My Life	87
35	Infusion Day #7	89
36	This is Going to be an Amazing Comeback	91

37	Quick Note of Gratitude	95
38	Infusion Day #8 – It is All About Love!	97
39	Infusion Day #9 – What is Loneliness?	101
40	"Good to See No Sign of Cancer"	105
41	It's a Miracle!	107
42	Infusion Day #10 – This is It!	109
43	I Don't Need Any Help! (Maybe I Do!)	111
44	Infusion Day #11 – Almost Done	113
45	Reframing the Day	115
46	Mini Epiphany	117
47	We All Want to Leave a Positive Impact on Others	119
48	Infusion Day #12 – Last One	121
49	What I Learned about Gratitude	123
50	What I Learned about Anger and Forgiveness	127
51	What I Learned about Love	131
52	Second Chances	135
53	What Can I Learn Today?	137
54	Yesterday, I Rang the Bell. Today, I am Just Tired	139
55	Afterword	141

About The Author — 145

Preface

As I sat down to write this, I had been in tears all day. I had just learned that my friend and coworker had passed away from the dreaded disease of cancer. She was a multitalented person, full of life and energy, and someone with whom I always enjoyed talking. We were both diagnosed at about the same time. I never imagined that someone like her could be taken so early, and I've had a sense of survivor's guilt since finding out. Why spare me and not her?

A few days earlier, in a meeting with my boss, I had explained that this person's health was deteriorating. She seemed to sense my feelings and in a stern voice, she told me not to go there. I had nothing to feel guilty about. She continued to remind me that I have worked hard to be in my position.

While I agreed with her, we don't know how cancer works and why it affects every person differently. Sometimes it seems like a lottery, with life-and-death outcomes. I do not think I could ever know the reasons why these things happen, but I do know that I miss my friend and our interactions. And at the same time, I feel truly blessed for being alive.

This may sound crazy to some, but could it be that we design our lives to have these challenges? If one believes in the eternal nature of the soul, is it possible that we design our lives and the challenges we face to learn from our experiences here on Earth, to grow and evolve as souls?

In this book, I am not asking the reader to believe what I do. I am only able to convey my personal learnings from my journey.

Introduction

When I was first diagnosed with Stage 3b colon cancer, I talked with a friend, and she suggested I write a journal about my experiences to publish. She told me that no matter what happened, my experiences could be valuable to someone going through the same or similar disease. I agreed and was immediately excited by the prospect, but life happened. I got busy at work, and this idea was on the back burner.

It wasn't until another friend told me about an organization called CaringBridge that the possibility of writing a journal of my experiences became a reality. CaringBridge is an online place where those who may have contracted a long-term illness such as cancer can create a website to keep family and friends updated on the status of their condition.

In addition to the personalized websites, many additional resources for assistance or coping can be found on CaringBridge to help those connected to the person with the illness. They say on the website that they want to "create a world where no one goes through a health journey alone."

The site was so easy to set up and use that it became a companion to me as I moved through this illness. I could write anything

I felt at the time and have friends and family comment or show their support for the challenges I was going through. My posts often became metaphysical, but I vowed to write whatever I felt. It was a great release for me. For that reason, I will be donating a portion of the net proceeds of this book to the CaringBridge organization.

Cancer is a strange disease that attacks each victim differently. For example, the five-year mortality rate for someone with my stage of cancer is approximately 50%. It is nothing more than a flip of a coin. Each person must rely on both intuition and research in approaching treatment. I can't tell you the number of times I was told that if I did X, Y, or Z, I would be cured. I am grateful to those who gave me suggestions because they came from love and concern for my health.

Primarily, I was very hung up on the question, "Is receiving chemotherapy the right course of action for me?" I went back and forth on this for quite a while. After my operation, I felt great, and the surgeon told me all visible cancer was removed. Why did I need to subject myself to injecting poisons into my body? It took me an extra month of trying three different oncologists until I got answers that fit. At that point, I had collected enough information that, in addition to the metaphysical treatment and lifestyle changes, I decided to add chemotherapy to my arsenal.

This book is primarily the tale of my six-month journey through the chemo treatment and documents the ups, downs, and what I learned. Looking back, I could not have anticipated the long-term effects of my treatment and how they would be a challenge even after the chemotherapy ended. In my mind, once the chemo ended everything would be back to normal, but when you pump poison into your body for six months, there will always be some leftover effects.

The title of this book comes from a dream in which I was holding a book with this title and a similar cover. I will add that sometimes beyond the mountains, there are often more mountains, but the skills learned in traversing one set of mountains will assist as you attempt to pass over the others.

It is not my intent to say that if you follow my path, you will be cured of any cancer you face. I already know this disease is too indiscriminate for me to even make that suggestion. But I hope you find courage in your challenges by reading my words. I hope you will not only find happiness beyond the obstacles in your life, but will find joy in everything you can learn while traversing your mountains.

I have organized this book mostly chronologically, and have added editorial comments in italics when appropriate.

As you read this book, I would ask you to pay particular attention to three themes woven into the fabric of my journal entries: gratitude, forgiveness, and most importantly, love. Looking back, those energetic threads provided the greatest learning for me.

I

How Did This Journey Begin?

MARCH 29, 2023

In November 2022, I traveled to Southeast Asia on business. I first visited Indonesia, and then after a weekend in Bali, I flew to Cambodia. On my last day there, while I was visiting a factory, I began to get stomach cramps. I passed it off as having eaten some food that did not agree with me, and then it was back to the airport for a short flight to Ho Chi Minh, Vietnam. But I was still feeling off for some reason.

That night, at 2:00 a.m., I woke up with a fever. I had some rapid antigen tests with me, and within fifteen minutes, I knew what I had been avoiding for two and a half years had finally caught up to me. I voluntarily isolated myself in my hotel room for over a week until I tested negative for COVID-19. In my mind, I determined that the cramps I felt in Cambodia were just a weird symptom of COVID-19, since my stomach didn't bother me until much later.

Before going on the business trip, I had booked a one-week vacation for the end of it. The day after I tested negative for COVID, I was on a plane to Siem Reap, home of the famous Angkor Wat temples. One of my purposes in going there was to attend a meditation retreat. At this fantastic retreat, I learned so much in such a short time and was also privileged to eat some of the most amazing Ayurvedic food, which was heaven – but which, in hindsight, did not process through my body as it should have.

I didn't fully realize how incredibly valuable the meditation lessons I learned were until a few days later.

When I left Siem Reap, I took a short flight to Ho Chi Minh to catch my flight to Seattle the following day. I was excited, as I would have a whole evening to go downtown to one of my favorite restaurants for dinner. But after checking into the hotel, my plans quickly changed.

I walked into the room, put down my bags, and immediately felt a pain in my stomach like never before. It was like something was hitting me in my lower abdomen. I thought it would be better not to venture far from the toilet, and I spent most of that night curled in a fetal position on the hotel bed. I could only alleviate the pain by using the profound meditation techniques I learned at the retreat.

By 3:00 a.m., the pain was still intense, and I began to worry that I would not make my morning flight. Thankfully, when I had to leave for the airport at 5:00 a.m., it had subsided a bit. I made it to my flight but only ate a little on the plane and on my layover at the

Narita Airport in Japan. I really love Japanese ramen, so not eating any at Narita was a big deal.

One week after returning to the States, I still had constant stomach pain. I noticed that as food entered my body, only a minimal amount left it. After consulting with a doctor on a telemedicine call, I decided to go to the ER. At the time, I believed the food of my travels was just constipating me. Each time I mentioned that to a doctor in the ER, they chuckled and said that if it were an issue with something I ate, I would actually be having the opposite problem.

A CT scan finally revealed that I had a tennis ball-sized tumor in my colon that was blocking it. The next day, I had an emergency procedure to place a stent in my colon to relieve the pressure.

Before that procedure, as the waves of pain would arrive, I once again fell back on the meditation techniques I had learned at the retreat. I remember thinking how fortunate I had been to attend the retreat when I did, not knowing then how it would so greatly help me manage this future pain.

I was discharged from the hospital on Christmas Eve. The following week, I met with a colorectal surgeon. The best course was to remove the section of my descending colon that included the tumor. We set a date for January 17th.

I had no reservations about the surgery until the night before. A wave of panic came over me as I lay in my bed. I worried about the surgery and whether any complications would arise. It was then that it hit me: I had cancer. Cancer is something other people have, but not me. Was this the beginning of the end of my life?

A deep despair began to overwhelm me. At that moment, I really felt anxious and hopeless. Just as everything seemed to hit the darkest point, I suddenly felt my mother's presence in my room. She had passed away in 2016, and since then, I have felt her spirit visit me on occasion. This was one of those times. She was accompanied by another spirit whom I wrote about in my first book.

I immediately felt at peace. I heard in my mind that everything would be okay. Then, something magical happened, and I cannot fully explain it to this day. It was almost like my mother pulled back what seemed to be a curtain that separates this life from the next, and allowed me to feel the unconditional love that emanated from that place. It felt like a very high-frequency vibration moved throughout my body, tingling all over.

At that moment, a sense of deep peace and calm enveloped me. I instantly knew everything would be okay. Just as quickly as it had come, it was gone, but the tranquility remained.

The next day, a very skilled surgeon removed the tumor and 33 cm of the colon. Thank goodness my sister, Karen, flew in from Philadelphia to take care of me that first week post-surgery. There were times when sneezing was an excruciating act. I was grateful for her sacrifice for me.

The surgeon had recommended adjuvant chemotherapy, stating that he had removed all visible cancer, but the chemo would be to ensure that anything that was not visible was also removed. As mentioned in the intro, I needed time before making my decision about chemo.

Over the course of a month I visited three different oncologists.

When I met with the first, I was not convinced that chemo was the best path for me. He did nothing to help, as he did not seem interested in my concerns. I got a second opinion at a major cancer institute in downtown Seattle. The doctor there explained the seriousness of my situation in a way that really made sense. Still, she suggested I get an oncologist closer to my residence to avoid the aggravation of the commute on top of the treatments.

After some calling, I finally got an appointment with my current oncologist. He was the right doctor at the right time, and he even understood my stupid jokes (bonus points). We scheduled six months of chemotherapy treatments to begin April 10th.

What follows is a diary of journal entries from my treatments.

2

My First Post

MARCH 29, 2023

I am not asking for anything more than your energetic support and good vibes. I hope to maintain this attitude as I move through this process.

This quote is from my first book, *Do You Hear My Voice? Discovering Jessica Again*, published in 2021:

> "Enjoy the ride! I am talking about every beautiful thing and action that you see, and the adversities you face. Being human is such a remarkable thing. One day, you will look back on it all and begin to comprehend the magnificence in all that you experience and how fortunate you have been."
> – Jessica

Looking back, I had no clue about the road ahead. In some ways, I *felt overly optimistic, but in other ways, I underestimated the love I would feel. Enjoying the ride is often more difficult when you do not feel healthy or strong. Trying to maintain optimism when all you want is to make it to the next day can be challenging.*

3

The First Step is Tomorrow

MARCH 31, 2023

I just got off the phone with the Infusion Center. They are moving things around to accommodate my work travel schedule. Part of the routine will be to get two sets of infusions. One will be at the hospital's Infusion Center, and that set of drugs will be given to me over two to three hours while I am there. A second drug will be given to me via slow drip over a 48-hour period. For that, I will need a mobile pump that I will wear in a fanny pack.

My new schedule is:

- April 3rd – Chemo port placement – I am lucky enough to get this new badge of courage
- April 4th – Chemo orientation – I feel like a new kid at school
- April 10th – My first cocktail at the Infusion Center (that

sounds so much better than it is, but that is what I am going with)
- April 12th – Disconnection of the mobile pump (I asked if I could do it myself, but they said they didn't want me messing things up)
- April 16th – Business trip to Boston
- April 25th – Second cocktail
- April 27th – Disconnection date

As if all that wasn't enough, I signed up for the "April 100 Mile Challenge" for the American Cancer Society. In hindsight, it was not the best decision I have ever made to commit to walking 100 miles in the same month I start chemotherapy. But through the generosity of some friends and family members, I have quickly surpassed my fundraising goal, so now I really feel I must do it.

Since I've surpassed that goal, I have been looking for ways my friends and family could join me on my walks, albeit virtually. If you have the desire to walk with me in spirit, please take a photo of your walk and tell me a little about it.

Tomorrow is the start of that journey for me. Unfortunately, the weather forecast for this weekend calls for a lot of rain, so I may be taking my first steps on a treadmill. Wherever you are, please join me. #WalkwithBruce

Lao Tzu said, "A journey of a thousand miles begins with a single step." In my case, it was a journey of one hundred miles, but I had no idea just how difficult some of those additional steps would be, the things I would learn, or the acts of extraordinary kindness that would be shown to me along the way.

4

Waiting is the Hardest Part

APRIL 3, 2023

Quick update. I have an appointment to install my infusion port at 1:30 today. Realizing we had a post office only half a mile away and a book I needed to mail to my cousin, I decided to feed two birds with one piece of bread. So, I added some mileage and walked to the post office.

Along the way, I listened to a book on Audible. It was an enjoyable walk, even though it was chilly for Puget Sound. The hospital is about a two-mile walk from here, so I plan to walk, and my daughter will pick me up after the procedure.

I remember showing up to the surgical center very sweaty from my walk. I wonder what the woman checking me in thought of the man wet from perspiration standing in front of her. Did she think I was really nervous about this minor procedure, or really sick?

5

A Metaphysical Post

APRIL 3, 2023

I just got home from having my chest port installed. As I was waiting in the pre-op room, the impact of what I would be doing for the next six months hit me. I felt what seemed like an enormous weight descend over me. It was the first time I had experienced that feeling throughout this whole process.

When I began to feel overwhelmed, I felt what seemed like golden energy slowly filling the room. In my mind, I heard that this was just a tiny portion of all the love, prayers, and good vibes being directed my way.

As much as I was overcome with the enormity of what was ahead, I was comforted with a calming sense of peace and serenity. Thank you so much to everyone sending me such positive vibes.

The feeling differed from what I had experienced the night before my surgery, but within it, I felt the love of those who cared for me. I wish I could bottle up that feeling and share it with others. It is different, wonderful, and oh-so-peaceful. I have talked to others who have been through the cancer process, and many have felt a similar feeling.

6

Feeling Gratitude

APRIL 5, 2023

This will probably be quick. Last night, I went to my chemo orientation and received a goodie bag. One of the items in the goodie bag was a hand-knit beanie. I put it on my head and took a selfie with my new beanie, hoping I would never have to use it because of lost hair. I sent the photo to a few friends, and one of them commented, "How special. Someone made that with so much love."

As I walked at lunchtime, I couldn't get that thought out of my mind. It was then I felt a wave of gratitude for that person, whoever they are, knitting the hat to give comfort and support to someone they may never meet.

Even today, I sometimes pull out that hat and marvel at the selfless love of its creator. Each time I do, tears come to my eyes as I feel gratitude for the person I will never meet who made that for me.

7

More Gratitude

APRIL 8, 2023

While walking today, I realized it had been ten years since a skillful surgeon replaced my old, damaged knee joints with titanium ones. As I continued to walk, I found a grassy pathway that led me to a small neighborhood park. That park was such a remarkable change of scenery, as up to this point, I had walked most of my 30 miles in the last week on a treadmill or an urban sidewalk. Walking through the park, it felt like I could almost breathe in the energy from all the plants and trees around me. It really gave me an energy boost to continue the walk.

Here is the funny thing. Without the skill of that surgeon ten years ago, I would not have been able to enjoy that park today. Did I experience an immense amount of pain after that surgery? Absolutely!

However, had I not gone through that pain, I would not have been able to enjoy that park today. I see many parallels to my path ahead. I am so grateful for the skills of those in the medical profession and the energy I receive from friends and family. I also understand that hardships bring about learning and progress, which is an important perspective for me on this journey.

This was probably the first post in which I explored my journey using a metaphor. Sometimes, a well-placed metaphor can explain things far better than I could. The reader may notice many more in the coming pages. Expressing my life this way allowed me to articulate what was happening in simpler terms.

8

First Cocktail – It's a "TrustFall"

APRIL 10, 2023

Well, today is my first day of chemo. I do not know how my body will handle this or how it will react. It is really a new adventure. My goal in writing in this journal is to be as open with what is happening to me as possible. Right now, I am two hours in and it hasn't been that bad, but my nurse also said it is generally two or three days after the initial infusion when most feel the worst side effects.

For now, I am just soaking in all that I can. I can tell you that I feel surrounded by love energy from so many on both sides of the veil. There is comfort in that.

By the way, the song of the day is P!nk's "Trustfall." When you think about it, going through chemo is so much like a trust fall as one closes their eyes, falls backward, and trusts that others will catch them. In my case, it would be the medical staff, friends, and family who will cushion my fall.

Funny, every time I hear that song now, I am immediately transported back to the infusion room, complete with all the emotions and feelings of that time. The song became such a big part of my infusion experience; it certainly marked transformative moments on my cancer journey. I still love the song, but for reasons other than I originally did. Music can be so magical in the way that it can transform moods. Throughout my journey, I really tried to focus on music that would inspire and teach me.

9

I am Sooo Tired!

APRIL 12, 2023

This will not be my most exciting post yet.

Chemo fatigue really hit me today. I didn't want to do anything except sleep and watch *Ted Lasso*. I did go to the Infusion Center to have my mobile pump removed. (I must only use it every other week.) The worst part of that experience was when the (maybe partially sadistic) nurse removed the tape securing the cover over my chest port and took all the chest hair with it. I vowed never to wax my chest or any other body part after that.

To ease my pain, I came home and had a big bowl of Frosted Mini-Wheats. It is the simple pleasures, right?

Well, back to bed for me. Today was exhausting.

One of the residual effects of chemo can be hard to describe. For several days following treatment, I would get pins and needles in my hands and feet, which were sensitive to hot and cold temperatures. Sometimes, just grabbing something from the refrigerator was an excruciating experience.

That sensitivity would also be present in my mouth and throat. I remember that while the Frosted Mini-Wheats tasted so good, I had to warm the milk to eat them.

10

Learning to Listen to My Body (and Others' Experiences)

APRIL 15, 2023

Wow! The last three days were definitely interesting. I already wrote about Wednesday, but I woke up feeling like a big truck ran me over in the middle of the night on Thursday. I could barely leave the bed to let Chipper (the dog) out and feed him. That poor little fellow, so whiny but so patient at the same time. I did work sporadically, but I took some naps in between.

Any extended walking was out of the question, but I have a wonderful boss who stepped in for me, took the baton, and walked the miles I could not. What a fantastic gesture!

Early on Friday morning, I woke up feeling lethargic, and questions began to fire in my head. "Can I really handle six months of this? Is this worth it? I wonder if anyone has quit after one week? Now that I am awake, will I be able to get back to sleep?"

I did go back to sleep and woke at about 7 a.m. to care for Chipper. After I had a cup of coffee, the fog from the previous days magically began to lift. I felt like I finally could join the living. I worked most of the day but was lightheaded each time I stood up. I did walk to the mailbox and back, but other than that, there was no actual walking.

That brings us to this morning. I woke up feeling great. I went to my favorite route-mapping website and mapped out a four-mile round trip, a distance that would have been doable just one week ago. I began walking, thinking, "This is great!"

Along the way it became less and less great, until, at the one-mile mark, I realized that four miles would not be feasible today. I decided to stick my proud tail between my legs and head back.

This was a smart decision, as the last half mile was primarily uphill. With my legs shaking, I made it home. I never would have made the entire route and would have gotten to a point where I could not have gone forward or back.

I have listened to many of you say, "Be kind to yourself and listen to your body."

I learned today to really appreciate that advice. I am now here to proudly exclaim, "I am grateful to be alive, and I walked a whole two miles without stopping at the end of my first week of chemo."

Off to Boston in the morning.

Later, I learned that they gave me a steroid with my dose of drugs that would last 48 to 72 hours, and that is why I would feel like I hit a wall two to three days after my initial infusions.

11

Boston

APRIL 17, 2023

What an enjoyable morning I had. Despite the travel and time zone change, I felt great this morning. I even got up at 5:30 a.m. (2:30 a.m. PST) and went on a 6:00 a.m. walk from the hotel to Boston Common.

The first bit of awesomeness happened when I got to the lobby and found my coworker waiting to join me on my walk. She was the first non-virtual walking companion I have had. Walking to the center of Boston was so fun, and it was amazing seeing American history along the way.

The second bit of awesomeness was to see some of the 30,000 Boston Marathon participants head to the same Boston Common to catch a school bus to the starting line. All looked so eager, but I noticed that many were already determined about the task ahead.

It was an excellent metaphor for me as I look at my upcoming marathon of a different kind.

Lesson #1 from Boston: **Focus on the goal, but enjoy the process.**

Finally, the third bit of awesomeness was when Dunkin' Donuts opened early in the morning.

Iced coffee and an apple fritter never tasted so good.

12

The Sun Comes Out

APRIL 18, 2023

> "You will have bad times, but that'll always wake you up to the good stuff you weren't paying attention to."
> – Robin Williams as Sean Maguire in *Good Will Hunting*

Everything is energy, right?

I am always amazed at how a vibe can change overnight. Yesterday was a misty and overcast holiday filled with focused marathoners. Today, it energetically changed to a vibrant working city, the focused determination of yesterday replaced with tasked-focused energy. The sky was clear, with the sun coming up. Construction workers headed toward their jobs at 6:00 a.m. The pace of the city changed from a long-distance run to almost a sprint.

This, too, was also an excellent metaphor for my life. Sometimes, one needs to be focused on the end goal, but other times, it is about doing what needs to be done in the short term to meet the long-term objectives.

Lesson #2 from Boston: **Sometimes it takes going in to get an infusion, knowing the after-effects will come, and other times it is about going for a walk to increase long-term overall health.**

13

Just Get Up

APRIL 19, 2023

I woke up this morning and had zero desire to walk. The old joints were hurting. Part of me was saying, "Stay in bed. You deserve it. You have been going through so much recently. No one will care if you take a break today. Everyone would understand."

Then, a voice from deeper within told me, "Get up!"

I got up slightly earlier than usual and was out the door by 5:30 a.m. The walk this morning was much chillier than it had been the past couple of days, with a brisk wind in my face. When I got to the bridge where I had previously taken a couple of photos, I decided to turn right, take a different route, and see where that would take me. My intuition did not disappoint.

I discovered a Holocaust memorial. The significance of that

place hit me hard, especially when much of the conference I have been attending deals with how companies can comply with the new Uyghur Forced Labor Prevention Act. The law states that purchasing and importing anything resulting from forced labor in that region is illegal. This becomes very challenging because we use so many elements daily that may have a strand of cotton or a piece of plastic produced there.

The Uyghurs are an ethnic group in China that is being targeted, forced into work camps, and often killed for nothing more than their ethnicity. I won't go into the details, but simply put, some scholars have compared much of what is happening in China now to what happened in Nazi Germany.

As I walked through that memorial today, I was struck by the significance of steam rising from the ground, representing each of the largest concentration camps. So many people were tortured and killed for nothing more than their ethnicity during that horrific time. The whys of that are too painful even to comprehend.

As I visited that location, I realized that what is happening in China now with the Uyghurs is on our watch. While the task seems overwhelming, how can I not do all I can to prevent history from repeating itself?

Compared to this, my medical issues seem minor. I know I can get through this.

Lesson #3 from Boston: **Get up and keep going.**

So much of my journey was learning to look at challenges with a new perspective. I didn't want to get up. I knew that my body already hurt, and

I knew that no one would blame me for taking a break – but on the other hand, think of what I would have missed had I not gotten up that day.

Writing this now, I think back to a time in my young adult life when I was ready to give up on life. I did not see any point in continuing. I had a gun held to my temple, and I sat there for a long time with my finger on the trigger. Finally, I lowered the gun because I didn't want anyone else to have to clean up my mess.

I ended up taking a copy of the anatomy book called Grey's Anatomy. It had a picture of a head on the cover. I discharged the gun into the book in an attempt to release some of my tension, and the bullet traveled only three-fourths of the way through the book. When I saw that, I vowed to never try that again. I kept that book with me for several years, and every once in a while, I would take it out to remind myself of all that I would have missed in my life had I gone through with that.

Ironically, during this whole journey, I fought so hard to save that same life I was trying to throw away back then. Sometimes amazing and magical moments exist just beyond the difficulties in life, and one just needs to get beyond the visible mountains to find them. At times, that requires us just to get up and keep going without being able to immediately see those things.

14

Feeling Good

APRIL 22, 2023

On my walk today, I asked my friend Siri for a fun playlist. What I got was one called, "Feeling Good." It is not one I would have chosen on my own, but it was the perfect one for me today. With artists like Dua Lipa, Lizzo, and Beyoncé, it definitely is not something I would generally listen to. Okay, yes, I am that old guy now.

As I listened to my playlist, I saw groups of children having a wonderful time playing soccer and t-ball. The kids looked like they were having so much fun. I passed a man walking his English bulldog, who must not have seen me because he jumped about a foot in the air when I said hello.

All this time, the playlist was playing songs that were really helping me feel good. Then, as I turned down a grassy pathway, a song came on called "You're Special," and I thought about all those who are so special to me and who have been so supportive.

Thank you for all your love and support.

15

Infusion Day #2 – Music

APRIL 25, 2023

It has been a very interesting day today. It is much easier when I know the routine. I am working and listening to music right now. Is there a better song than Earth, Wind, and Fire's "September" to make you feel good?

Other impactful songs today:

- Queen's "These Are the Days of Our Lives" is a melancholy song that came on halfway through the infusion at the hospital.
- Joe Cocker's "The Moon is a Harsh Mistress" talks about the pain that sometimes comes with learning to love.
- Probably one you have never heard, Victoria Tolstoy's "Love is Real," is about true love being pure and right.

As some of you know, I am writing another book now. It is a fictitious story of a man being taught by an angel what love really is. Two themes have evolved from the story. First, love is real. Second, we all come to Earth to learn how to love and be loved, despite hardships and difficulties. In fact, it is those adversities that are our greatest teachers. I am really excited to share the whole story soon.

By the way, my nurse today, Marta, has been excellent! She even gets my stupid jokes, or pretends to get them. Everyone I have met here has been so caring.

Music can be such a powerful force. Many times, it was the music that accompanied me through the journey. When I felt sad, lonely, or even frustrated with the process, music became my companion to soothe my heart.

Conversely, music became a friend to celebrate with during my victories and those times of spiritual insight. I could almost tell my entire story by the music I would listen to on any particular date.

16

100 Miles! (We Did It!)

APRIL 25, 2023

I just looked at the pedometer on my watch, did a few calculations, and realized that I had passed the 100-mile mark for April. Keep this in mind: I didn't do this on my own. The energy I felt from so many of you helped me take that extra step when I didn't feel I had it in me.

However, I want to call out one particular person: my boss, Kandace. Two weeks ago, when the first round of chemo kicked my butt, she told me, "I've got this," and for three days she picked up the baton I had dropped and walked on my behalf. I proudly included her miles in my total.

I will continue walking and would love to have my walking companions with me until I am cancer-free.

When I realized that I had completed the 100 miles, it was such a relief. I was feeling myself getting weaker with each infusion and honestly did not know how I would be able to continue.

Additionally, each time I reflect on the gift my boss gave me, I am filled with an immense sense of gratitude. She did not have to do that, but because of the compassion in her heart, she did. Throughout this whole process, that kindness would be demonstrated repeatedly.

17

Oh Well!

APRIL 29, 2023

I am losing my hair! It will be interesting to see where this goes. I had a dream last night that this was happening. My oncologist had told me that 90% don't lose hair with my kind of chemo. I'm shedding like a golden retriever.

I finally gave up and decided to shave it and save the agony of watching the slow attrition.

I am not a good-looking bald man. Many men can pull it off and look great, but not so much with me. Losing my hair seemed traumatic to me. I never expected it, as the oncologist had stated the likelihood was small.

I realize it is pure vanity. It must seem ridiculous for someone fighting cancer to be so worried about losing hair, but I became a hat man even after my hair began to come back.

It seems to be a greater symptom of not wanting to admit to even myself that I had cancer.

18

Changing Focus

MAY 2, 2023

Yesterday, I received a reminder of my next infusion appointment. When I saw it, my spirit sank. This last week was more difficult for me than the first, and the thought of going through the process ten more times felt more than I could bear.

At about that time, a dear friend contacted me requesting assistance. Did she really need my help? Probably not. Was she inspired to reach out to me at that time? Absolutely!

Sometimes in life, magic happens. As I was thinking of and working on her request, I felt connected to that universal and all-inclusive love I wrote of before; I really wish I could package and share it. Simply put, it is very intense, encompassing, and comforting.

After experiencing that, how many chemo treatments I had to receive, or any detrimental side effects I had to endure, seemed inconsequential. We are all part of that love, and I was lucky to experience it again yesterday.

Here's to inspired friends.

Would it surprise you if I told you that the last name of that friend is Angel?

19

Expressing Gratitude

MAY 4, 2023

Today, I was again reminded just how important it is to express gratitude. After working with a coworker in a different department, I thought, "I really like working with her."

I would probably not have mentioned it, but something in me said, "Tell her!"

So, I did. That simple act made my day as much as it did hers, as we were both able to express something that had not been previously mentioned – that we enjoy working together.

With that experience, I thought about this journal and how wonderful it has been having a location to express my feelings as I move through this journey. I remembered all of you who have followed, liked, commented, or just dropped in to check on me. My heart is filled with tremendous, special gratitude for each of you for the care, love, and concern you have shown me.

Thank you all for being part of my journey.

It is one thing to feel gratitude, but it's equally important to express it. Gratitude often makes you and others feel great, so why not share the happiness?

20

Infusion Day #3 – Making Adjustments

MAY 9, 2023

Quick message today.

Platelets were low this morning but not too low. The oncologist reduced my dosage, and we are moving forward.

When I thought of what the doctor did, I realized it was an excellent metaphor for life. When life gets difficult, don't quit; make sound adjustments and move on.

So much of life is not about avoiding the obstacles but finding our way through.

Hmm! Where have I heard that before?

Interestingly, to give you some idea of how much damage chemotherapy can do, it took nearly 8 months following the completion of my chemo for my platelets to creep back to the normal value.

Have you ever seen a farmer burn his field to plant a new crop? It is almost like that.

21

Caution: Another Metaphor Coming

MAY 14, 2023

Last weekend, I was in my hometown for my daughter's college graduation. One afternoon, we drove upriver to see how much water was in the reservoirs behind several dams. (I know, I'm weird, but I did it as a kid.)

While there, I photographed myself standing before one of those dams. I have kept returning to that photo this week, each time thinking of what a remarkable metaphor it is. To explain that, I must tell another story.

Everyone's experience is so different. I can only speak to myself. As I pondered my rehabilitation, I realized the first thing I needed to heal was the energetic causes.

One of the things I have learned through this process is that besides the dietary, biological, and environmental causes of my cancer, there are also energetic causes. Remember, I am not speaking for cancer in general, but specifically with my cancer.

Luckily, I have a good friend, Molly, who is a fantastic bio-energy healer. Working with her, we discovered areas where I was holding on to deeper emotional blockages. These blockages stemmed from self-anger and self-criticism. I found I was very judgmental of the decisions I made in my life, more so than any other person would be. I was my own biggest critic. I looked with disdain at each decision, feeling I could have done better. And I held all that in, creating stress in my body.

When I could finally begin to release those emotions and forgive myself, something in me changed. As I slowly released that anger, I found in its place kindness and self-compassion for all those times when I didn't measure up to my own intentions or expectations.

So, what's the metaphor? When I released my internally dammed-up emotions, I found only kindness and love.

Recently, I have been reading a lot of literature on studies of emotions on overall health. Sometimes, we like to view the physical body and emotional body as two separate entities. They are, in fact, so very intertwined, and we must work hard to not only keep both in shape, but in balance.

22

Infusion Day #4

MAY 23, 2023

Today, I realized just how thankful I am to be here in the Infusion Center. There are so many medical professionals who not only treat me with respect but also with care, compassion, and an occasional joke.

I know that there are nurses and other medical workers who follow this blog. Please accept my heartfelt gratitude for all that you do.

During this whole process, I gained such a respect for those who are in the medical profession. I experienced so many acts of compassionate service throughout my journey.

Before my initial procedure to remove the blockage from my colon, the Seattle area had faced a rare ice storm, and the car of one of my nurses slid off the road on the way to work. Instead of calling in sick, he abandoned his car and walked the remainder of the way because he knew the hospital was short-staffed due to the storm. Because of his selfless act, I received the care I needed.

That is just one of many beautiful examples of the amazing care given by the medical professionals I worked with.

23

Hibernation

MAY 28, 2023

Since Friday morning, I have spent so much time just sleeping. It is almost like chemo really caught up to me. My challenge has been to release the guilt around doing nothing but sleeping. I am still working on that, as I have a long to-do list.

I have had some interesting dreams, though. In one, I was at a team building event at one of our distribution centers. I had mentioned earlier to the Director how impressed I was with the change in energy in the building. Everyone sat in a big circle at the activity and talked about Christmas celebrations. Suddenly I stood up, wearing an old pair of bib overalls. I said, "I come from stoic Wisconsin dairy farmers where hard work was more prized than celebration."

The message for me was that I could have fun now, celebrate successes, and not cling to past patterns.

In another dream, I was somewhere in Northern Europe in a library. We were playing a game I didn't understand, but I was having great fun. The game had many people divided into several groups. In some respects, it seemed like a drinking game, but with books. When it came to each group's turn, they would pick up a book and in unison, read the book's name aloud, say a chant I never got or understood, and finish by chanting loudly, "OOYA! OOYA! OY! OY! OY!"

To me, the dream was hinting that I would have fun writing and should not look upon it as a chore.

The last dream that had an impact was also rather touching. I entered a tattoo/piercing shop in Asia somewhere, carrying a bag with a small modern-day kayagum on my back. I immediately recognized the receptionist as someone I had worked with.

When she saw me, she seemed so happy and began to tell everyone a story about something I had done. She had been booked on passage to another country to obtain work, but somehow, I had discerned that she was about to be sold into slavery. Evidently, I sold my priceless kayagum, which I loved and was the source of my income, to buy her freedom.

What did this dream mean to me? Kindness never goes unnoticed and it actually can change lives.

If you read my first book, you will know what an impact dreams have had on my life. I continue to find them fascinating and incredibly insightful tools for learning about myself. I have often heard that when someone faces difficulty or deals with a significant illness, dreams can provide comfort, guidance, or insight to assist the dreamer in finding strength or overcoming challenges.

I really felt that to be what was happening in my dreams, but just to be sure, I recently asked my friend April Angel to help me understand the deeper meaning of these dreams. April is an excellent dream interpreter and teacher who is working with Michael Sheridan at Aisling Dream Interpretation.

When she looked at the first dream, she identified that I was receiving an energy upgrade during this time. She said that Christmas is a birth celebration, and the dream was telling me I need to remember to celebrate my birth and my life on this planet, and not be so focused on valuing work over joy. The cancer experience has put me face to face with life to examine what is true. It is clear there is more joy in life than I had been conditioned to grant myself, and part of my journey was to learn how to open up to that.

She brought up an additional point about the circle of people in that dream, and the symbolism is so beautiful that I had to quote it: "There is God in all things. Circles can represent God in dreams, as there is no beginning and no end. Everyone is sitting in a big circle in this dream, meaning there is God in all of us. We are God expressing Itself when you bring your attention to notice. You were feeling this more truly during the trial to reclaim your life and health."

Imagine the elegance of that statement. We are all expressions of God, and we just need to bring our attention to that to notice it. This reminds me of an experience I wrote of in my first book, when I was meditating and for a short period of time, "I felt so connected to humanity and the energy of all on this Earth in a way that I never have before. My very existence depended on everyone else's. For that moment, there was no separation."

It was such a powerful thing to experience, and I never forgot that.

The second dream was also reminding me to have fun and celebrate life and accomplishments with others, according to April: "This dream is given to lift your spirits and help you understand how much support and cheering is done on the other side of life, despite the experiences here and because of the experiences here. You are getting to experience this for yourself in the dream during a low time. It is a healing device to help you feel better. Dreams can do this when life feels particularly grueling."

As I said before, dreams sometimes help us lift ourselves during our most difficult times.

The final dream was truly touching and through April's interpretation, provides more depth of understanding around why my mother's spirit visited me to provide comfort prior to my initial surgery.

April wrote that foreign lands in dreams symbolize past lives, and tattoo shops represent life stories. So, this dream was telling me a story from a past life. Receptionists in dreams are always about one's reception in life or birth. In this case, April felt the receptionist represented my mother. An infant can often recognize a parent's energy, especially if they have shared a past life with that soul. In the dream I recognized the receptionist as someone I had "worked with," meaning I knew we had a deeper soul connection.

The act of me saving the receptionist from slavery was fairly significant, as I had to sell something dear to me to obtain her freedom. This is the kind of act that gets celebrated in the spirit world. April wrote that in order to repay my kindness in that life, my mother volunteered to give me life in this one, and it was an extreme honor for her to do that: "She agreed to give you life so you could continue to learn about and celebrate love, and in fact celebrate who you are."

Could it be that when my mother came to me before my surgery, she was continuing with her mission to remind and teach me about love in this life?

24

Pre-Sleep Vision

MAY 31, 2023

As I fell asleep last night, a vision of a light sculpture popped into my head. Thanks to the magic of AI, I was able to reproduce what it looked like, keeping it as a constant reminder and visualization tool. I got the feeling this is called "my healing tower."

Its base has golden, energetic lights symbolizing the love, prayers, and healing vibes I have received from many of you. The blue lights that top this tower of flowing energy represent all the blessings I have received, the lessons I have learned, and the increased gratitude I have felt.

I've got a long way to go, but seeing this filled my heart with joy.
But wait, there's more. I think this structure is not meant to be observed from the outside, but felt from within.

If you are curious, do you want to try an experiment? Close your eyes and envision yourself standing within a circle of lights, blue on top and golden on the bottom. See how you feel. It might be surprisingly healing.

Prayers are an interesting concept that I would have discounted before this journey. I have always equated them with religion, and for much of my adult life, I have tried to distance myself from any organized religion. I have since discovered that prayers go far beyond any religion and touch on the divine in each of us.

I am still not convinced that they can be a substitute for stepping in and helping someone, but they can effectively aid the healing process.

25

Infusion Day #5

JUNE 6, 2023

Just a quick note. I am not sure how this happens in this cosmic world in which we live. I have many friends who have no idea about my infusion schedule. How does it happen that many of them will contact me randomly on my infusion days?

I know it isn't planned based on the conversation or questions they ask, but every time it happens, it brings me joy. I know there may be days when it may not happen, but I am so thankful for those random texts when I need them the most.

This happened throughout the entire process. Someone whom I had not heard from in a long time would suddenly text me randomly as I sat hooked up to the machines in the Infusion Center. This was definitely not a coincidence!

26

Side Effects

JUNE 7, 2023

Warning: This is long but has a great metaphor in the end.

For all my positivity, I have days and nights like this. Yesterday, I went to the Infusion Center. Upon arrival, they checked my vitals and plugged tubing into a port in my chest connected directly to my vascular system. The nurse and I then had a lengthy conversation about all the side effects I had experienced since my last visit. Then I waited about an hour while my blood was analyzed, and my oncologist reviewed the results before giving the go-ahead for the day.

The nurse then begins the infusion process by giving me anti-nausea medication. This is followed by saline injections, which she pumps in and pulls back several times to ensure the blood is connected through the chest port. Next comes the injection of steroids and other IV fluids.

At this point, the nurse suits up in a protective gown and double gloves. Oxaliplatin is considered a dangerous poison to touch or be exposed to, so extra protection is needed as they are exposed to these poisons daily. I must remember that the job of these drugs is to kill any remaining cancer cells hanging around. I call this part the "love bombing." While I appreciate all that the cancer cells have taught me, I am trying to send them back to normal lovingly. Remember that sometimes, part of love is discipline when something is out of control.

Then I wait two hours for all the oxaliplatin to be loaded into my body. I am then disconnected from that drug, only to be hooked to a portable pump in a fanny pack containing fluorouracil. This is sometimes written as "FU." I have nicknamed my mobile pump Frank Underwood, after the despicable character in *House of Cards* on Netflix. During the changeover, the nurse again suits up in the protective gown.

This process has been the same the last five times, so why am I awake at 2:00 a.m. writing this? Today, it has been a combination of several things. On the way home, I stopped at the supermarket to buy a few things, as I knew I probably would not want to go for the next several days.

While there, I noticed the regular pins and needles feeling in my fingertips every time I touched something cold, which was unpleasant. Suddenly, the inside of my nasal passage began to hurt. It was something I had experienced once before, but this time, it seemed excruciating. Fluid flowed out my nose and down the back of my throat. I began sneezing.

That only lasted a few seconds, but then I got it under control. I purchased my goods and went home. I ate lunch, and then, without warning, I felt a lot of fluid moving from my sinuses down the back of my throat, and I began coughing. This cough continued, and I constantly had to clear the mucus from my throat to continue breathing properly.

This was uncomfortable and something that I've had to deal with throughout chemo regularly. It's only happened to a minor degree before. But this time, it seemed much worse, and I was unsure if it was my lunch or the drugs, but I became nauseated.

I took some nausea and nerve pain drugs, but suddenly, I found myself vomiting into the porcelain god in the bathroom. This was my first real experience of vomiting while in chemo, and not to get too graphic, my aim was not so good, so after I completed my session I cleaned the toilet and the surrounding areas with some bleach-based cleaner. The bathroom looks terrific, but it wasn't a great experience.

Now I am in bed trying to sleep while constantly worrying about the post-nasal drip. I'm also trying to be conscious of not lying on my left side since the other day I had some acid reflux that went into my nasal passage. Trust me, that's not a pleasant experience.

So why am I telling you all this? Do I want you to feel sorry for me? Am I just looking for attention? I realize that with positivity, there is also some element of pain, and how I handle the pain can make all the difference. If I look at the pain as "Woe is me," what will I learn? If I look at it as a learning experience or a means to an end, what can I learn from that?

I recently had a dream where I was told I needed to write a

new book called *Beyond the Mountains*. I thought that was a perfect metaphor for this cancer struggle. That is what I'm trying to do; I'm trying to move beyond the battle of cancer. So, these side effects are just part of the journey to my destination.

The title of this book has been such a powerful tool for me to visualize, not only seeing the end goal but also understanding that the journey itself is where life happens.

27

Does It Really Suck?

JUNE 8, 2023

Just a quick thought:

On the way home from the Infusion Center, the car in front of me moved to the other lane, and suddenly I found myself behind a vehicle with giant bold letters on the back window:

CANCER SUCKS

I was struck by the bold letters and started questioning, "Does it really suck?"

I would imagine if you have been dealing with it for over two years like my friend, have lost someone close to you, or have watched as a loved one deteriorated, it would suck. I know the medical treatment one receives definitely does suck. It is draining, and as one loses their hair and stomach contents, it can be demoralizing.

However, I can only speak for myself, as everyone is different. There are moments of complete clarity when you realize that you are mortal with a finite time on the planet, and then everything comes into alignment, making all the pain and suffering worth it.

My life has become more evident, my priorities have changed, and if I have six months or sixty years left here, I look forward to all I can learn because, ultimately, I believe we are here to learn and love.

That's it.

Does cancer suck? Absolutely, but there is so much more to learn in the process.

I am going to insert something that may be controversial to some. If one believes in reincarnation, is there a chance that we design the lives we want to live and the challenges and learning processes we want from that life? Throughout this whole journey, I have had the feeling that somehow, I planned to have cancer at this point in my life.

What I have learned in the process has been life-changing. Because of my cancer experiences, I feel so much closer now to the kind of person I was meant to be.

Crazy, right?

28

Yes, This is it! This is One Thing I Have Learned

JUNE 9, 2023

> "Sometimes when you're in a dark place you think you've been buried, but you've actually been planted."
> – Christine Caine, Australian activist

I don't remember where I saw this quote, but it appeared on a day that I really needed to read it. It is so elegant, yet so precise.

When things seem dark, I come back to this quote. Sometimes, when life seems to be at its darkest point, we are just beginning to grow. How cool is that visual?

29

I am Slowly Dying

JUNE 11, 2023

I recently received a call from a friend. As I answered the phone, his first question was, "How are you doing?"

I paused momentarily and responded, "I am slowly dying."

With some concern in his voice, my friend asked, "What's going on?"

I chuckled and said, "Yeah, from the time I was born, I have been slowly dying."

We only have a finite time here on Earth from the moment we are born. I know many who fear leaving this place, as this life is all they know, but I have seen more who fear what happens when their time is up. When we die, is it the end? Will we face judgment, or could this life be just one chance to learn more, and we will be returning?

Whatever it is, we are all slowly dying. How much time is on the clock, we do not know. I think one can find freedom in the fact that this life will inevitably end. Because of that, we are free to actually live.

From the time of my diagnosis, one song has constantly gone through my head. Any ideas? If you guessed Tim McGraw's "Live Like You Were Dying," you are right. There is much truth in that song.

There is a line in there that gets to me every time. In essence, it talks about giving forgiveness that you have been holding back. When I heard that after learning of my cancer, I began to think of the countless people I have not really forgiven. I thought about those who have used me as a stepping stone in their own careers and mistreated me. What about the guy who cut me off in traffic? I thought about my parents, whom I had never forgiven for being imperfect. And had I ever really forgiven myself for not being perfect, either?

We are all flawed, each with our own scars. In this life, we will never understand the scars another wears. If that is the case, can't one scarred person forgive another?

If we have one day left or 25,000 days, can we not start today to forgive?

I cannot stress how important this concept is. To forgive is to free your soul. It really doesn't matter if the one you forgive ever apologizes. The act of doing it will free you, and that is what matters most.

Holding on to any negative feelings toward yourself or others could possibly damage your health. Trust me.

30

Honoring My Body

JUNE 17, 2023

This week, I will be halfway through my chemo. I took the week off work to honor my body and give it additional time to heal and recover. Sadly, as much as I would like to act like I can do everything I previously could before chemo, this body that has had poisons dumped into it for nearly three months needs more recovery time. I have slept so much in the past week, but with all the sleep comes reflection.

I've been thinking of some of the monumental things that have happened in the past six months, and one of the most important things I did happened prior to my cancer diagnosis. That decision occurred in September of last year, but the event didn't happen until November: I thought that if I would be in SE Asia for three weeks on business, why not take an extra week of vacation and do something I have never done before?

So, I signed up for a meditation retreat in Siem Reap, Cambodia, the retreat I referenced earlier in this book.

As I was scheduled to be picked up for my retreat at noon, I decided to visit Angkor Wat at sunrise. Even though I had been there a few times before, I had never seen it at sunrise. What a beautiful experience despite all the other tourists. I felt a connection to those who lived there nearly 900 years ago. After roaming around for several hours, I returned to my hotel and waited to be picked up for my retreat.

A tuk-tuk picked me up, and when I arrived I felt underwhelmed, as it was on the 2nd and 3rd floors of an industrial-looking building. I checked in and was given a schedule for the following days. Krishna, the owner, was very cordial, and his wife, Bhawani, was a fantastic Ayurveda practitioner and cook. The meals there were terrific.

While my instructor practiced Pancha Kosha and taught much around that philosophy, we focused considerably on Pranayama or breathing. I spent significant time practicing breathing as we did our yoga exercises.

One lesson we learned was how to isolate and reduce pain. That concept benefited me in the future in ways I couldn't have imagined at the time. While there have been many times of pain when those practices helped, I was shocked most recently when my pump was removed.

They had taken my blood pressure, which was elevated to about 140/100. This nurse told me to relax for a moment, and then she would take it again. I immediately settled into the breathing I had learned. A few minutes later, when rechecked, it was 112/76. The nurse was shocked and commented she had never seen such a dramatic change in such a short time.

In my mind, I just said, "Thanks, Krishna."

Meditation can be an amazing tool. I must get better at making it a daily practice and not using it only as needed. When I have made it a constant practice, my life improves. During this journey, the elementary level I learned had an exponential effect on my pain tolerance.

31

Vulnerability

JUNE 18, 2023

Sitting here on my first Father's Day alone, I just watched this video by P!nk on YouTube. In the video, she talks about how vulnerability means a person can be wounded, and her implication seems to be that it is okay. She continues to indicate that she has made being vulnerable her life's objective. She also expressed gratitude for being alive, and for what she gets to do with this life.

My life has been blessed as I have become more vulnerable in front of you. I am a better person because of that. Thank you so much for going on this ride with me.

As a man, I have always struggled with the concept of vulnerability. I always viewed it as a sign of weakness, especially in the workplace. Admitting I have imperfections seemed like giving the enemy another weapon to tear me down. Why would I want to do that?

But why can't we flip the switch to make vulnerability in men a positive trait? I am not suggesting that men become vulnerable all the time, but there are times when it is okay to show that side. It engenders true connection and compassion from our fellow humans.

I have been more fulfilled as a human on this Earth when I have broken through those fears. I was able to touch on the essence of who we all are as souls, which is that we're loving beings just trying to make our way on this planet.

32

Infusion Day #6 – What a Lucky Day!

JUNE 20, 2023

Yes, I had another infusion, which might result in both expected and new side effects. Yes, I learned of a new side effect: oral thrush. Who knew that was a thing?

Yes, it is raining in Seattle. Yes, I do feel weak and lightheaded. But....

Today was full of delightful surprises:

- As I was getting ready to go to the hospital, I found an old lottery ticket that revealed I won $200 when scanned.
- I discovered $10 in my pocket when I put on my rain jacket.
- I was assigned my first male nurse, Nick, a young father who

took his kids camping and fishing on Father's Day. It was great talking to him about his kids and their adventures.
- When I returned home, I grabbed the mail. In the first envelope, I found a check for $120 from an overpayment to a company with which I do some business.
- When I opened the next envelope, I found a birthday card with $50 in it.

How lucky am I today?

Yes, chemo sucks, but sometimes the Universe gives me days like today to remind me what/who (depending on your belief system) is in charge of my life.

Sometimes, the Universe rewards you to let you know there is still a little magic in the world. It can be a call or text from a friend, or hearing a young father recount his Father's Day fishing adventures with his kids, or in my case, unexpected money.

Whatever it is, it really bumps up the needle on the gratitude scale.

33

"If/When" Will Never Make Me Happy

JUNE 22, 2023

Today, I had my chemo pump disconnected for the sixth time. As I am scheduled for 12 chemo sessions, I am halfway through chemotherapy. I was thinking about it this morning, and how happy I'll be when the chemo is all done.

Within 30 minutes of that thought, I received links from two friends with podcasts dealing with happiness. I am sure I will not do them justice, but my takeaway from both is this: When we look to the future and think, "If/when this happens, I will be happy," or "If this doesn't happen, I will be devastated," we will never truly be happy. We must find happiness in the present to find that elusive goal.

One of the podcasts was more metaphysical and spiritual. It discussed manifesting, and what happens when trying to manifest something that never happens. The speaker is an actress who was trying to manifest this new role she wanted, but when she didn't get it, many more positive opportunities started appearing.

Her message was, "May the best manifest." She didn't get the role she wanted, but the best did manifest in the end.

The other podcast featured a Yale professor who teaches a class on happiness. She directly talked with survivors of cancer and other traumas, who are actually some of the happier people around because they know that going through the ordeal has enriched their lives.

This led me to think about the two books I am writing. The first deals directly with my cancer journey. The other is a fiction novel about an angel who visits a young man whose life is off track. The angel visits for seven consecutive nights, each time teaching him about a new aspect of love. It is called *What She Said to Me*.

Trust me when I say I have no idea what will come out each time I sit down to write the second book. It seems to be a form of channeling energy from a different dimension, and if one has not experienced it, it may be difficult to understand. But I have heard of many musicians and writers who have had similar experiences.

One of the main themes in the second book seems to be that we do not want to avoid traumas and hardships, because by going through them, we can ultimately find so much love and happiness.

I guess this is just a long way of saying the Universe is amazing, and sometimes synchronicities can teach us so much if we are open to them. In my case today, the message was clear: "Enjoy the process more than the end game."

After I finished my chemo treatments, I was lucky enough to attend a Coldplay concert. H.E.R. opened for them. She has an amazing song called "The Journey." In the song, she sings of how life is not about arriving at the destination, but about the journey to get there. This song still resonates with me today. That is such an amazing sentiment.

34

The Duality of My Life

JUNE 26, 2023

Yesterday, my ex-brother-in-law and niece were in town to march in the Pride parade. I planned to head to the parade's end to view it and watch them march. By the time I made it through the traffic, parking in downtown Seattle was nearly nonexistent as I faced a mass of cars and people. My niece called me to say they were finished and ready to go. Luckily, I was still driving around and was able to pick them up curbside.

We decided to go to West Seattle for lunch. We had a great conversation while stuck in traffic for an hour, just trying to get out of the downtown core. We finally made it to the restaurant Marination Station, a great Korean/Hawaiian fusion restaurant with an incredible view across Elliott Bay to downtown Seattle. The food was terrific.

Feeling good, I drove around Alki Beach, and we ended up at Lincoln Park to take a post-lunch walk. We enjoyed walking through a forested area and then down to the beach. Now, here is where the duality comes in. As we walked down a slight decline to the beach, I suddenly felt my legs get rubbery and began worrying about our ascent out.

We had fun on the waterfront, and then it was time to leave. As the three of us started our climb back to the car, I warned my niece and her dad that I might need to stop a few times, complaining I couldn't believe just how weak I had become. My sweet niece put it into perspective. She said they had been dumping poison in my body for the last three months, and told me to take as much time as needed.

The duality comes from having a wonderful day with two people I love, while still dealing with the effects of chemo.

Would I give up either part of the duality? No! Why? On the one hand, I had a great day with people I adore. On the other, I witnessed the care and compassion of those same two people when I was struggling.

It all comes down to being seen and understood. On that day, I could not keep up with them, but did they act like I was imposing on them? Not at all. In essence, the message I felt that day was, "We see you, understand your challenges, and accept you no matter what."

The symbolism of the fact that they were both in town to march in the Pride parade was not lost on me. Sometimes, all we need is someone to tell us they see and accept us exactly as we are.

35

Infusion Day #7

JULY 4, 2023

I am sitting in the Infusion Center on Independence Day getting the seventh course of poisons injected into my body. I visited my oncologist on Tuesday, and he confirmed that I am on track. Good news, right?

Then, we discussed what would happen going forward and the process after the chemo ends. It didn't feel like freedom.

Up until then, I had been so focused on getting through the chemo as the end goal. Oh, but there is so much more. My heart sank when he mentioned that it would take two years to be considered cancer-free. My three months suddenly became two years and three months. I honestly didn't know if I had the strength and courage to last that long to finally be declared cancer-free.

It really sent me into a mini-depression, and this usually optimistic guy was suddenly not so hopeful. Thoughts of whether it was worth the effort to fight this crept in. I felt hopeless for a few days, and being a guy, I only knew that I didn't want to burden anyone with my fears and despondency.

Luckily, within a few days I was able to work my way out of it, and now I have the conviction and resolve to fight for however long it takes.

It is one thing to contemplate the future, but as I mentioned earlier, "if/when" doesn't really exist, as all we have is the present. Even knowing this, it is amazing how I still slip into that old pattern and worry about what might be or how long it will take, when I should be focusing on what I can do today.

Yes, there will be many more tests, but that is the process. A much better focus might be what I can learn and how I can grow today.

36

This is Going to be an Amazing Comeback

JULY 12, 2023

Let me preface by saying I'm not a Patriots or Brady fan. Still, tonight, I watched *80 for Brady* on Amazon Prime. In the movie, a main character named Luella, played by Lily Tomlin, has cancer. She's anticipating bad results from recent tests but decides to go to the Super Bowl with her three friends. As with any comedy, there are many mishaps, and when things look bleakest, she sees Tom Brady on a video board, talking about a "comeback mindset."

In her mind, she imagines him talking to her. Brady says that when things are a struggle, one needs to shift their mindset to say, "This is going to be an amazing comeback," and it will become a defining moment in life. He says that shift in mindset is empowering.

As I watched this, his words hit me hard. This last week has been one of the most difficult of my chemo experiences. I experienced constant nausea, my head was no more than a place for peach fuzz to grow, and my immune system and body were at their weakest points.

It is strange where inspiration can show up, but I am increasingly determined not to give up hope, and to make this a defining moment of my life.

And it is not lost on me that Lily Tomlin's character's name is Luella, which was my grandmother's name. Connection? Hmmm.

Sitting at my keyboard nearly a year later, I'm reflecting that it really has been an amazing journey. I look back at stories like this and realize that I was hoping I would become a survivor, but at that time, it was more of a hope than a belief. Now, I can feel it more and more as a reality.

There is something to be said about faith, just like prayer. I have always perceived those terms as mainly religious terms, and so I rebelled from them for most of my adult life.

I may need to parse my words carefully here: I believe that this thing called "spirituality" is a very big tent, as are the ideas of love and acceptance. Does any religion, sect, or spiritual belief have exclusive rights to these terms and beliefs?

Faith and prayer seem to have special powers, especially when combined, and are larger than any one belief system. I have no empirical evidence other than to say I have experienced the result of them both being directed toward me. I have felt the prayers viscerally, and they allowed me to have more faith that I would come out of this whole experience a better person.

As I write these words, I just realized that the reason they may work is because the power behind them is love. Without it, would faith and prayers really have any power?

37

Quick Note of Gratitude

JULY 15, 2023

Sometimes, I wallow in self-pity and forget to see the beauty around me. Some of those bright spots are each one of you. I really appreciate those of you following my journey and offering a click on the "heart" icon or making a quick comment of encouragement. I cannot begin to tell you what each of those means.

There have been many difficult days when I go back through some of the old posts and read the comments. It really helps me get through those days. Thank you for allowing me to share my journey with you, and for encouraging me along the way.

When I posted on CaringBridge, it was open for comments. Many friends, family members, and work colleagues from over the years supported me.

Some of the most powerful comments were from those who had led the way. They were cancer survivors whom I know had faced some of the same questions, doubts, and struggles with this disease, but they survived. While I valued all the comments and likes, some of the comments I trusted the most were from those who had already traveled the path.

38

Infusion Day #8 – It is All About Love!

JULY 18, 2023

So many thoughts are going through my head right now. This afternoon, I spent an hour and a half on the phone talking with a friend from college whom I hadn't spoken to in years. Ten years ago, he had a near-death experience and was clinically dead for 25 minutes. During that time, he visited the other side of the veil.

If you know me and have read my first book, you will know I have also had some fantastic metaphysical experiences. While I didn't die, I have been blessed to experience things on the other side. As we discussed our experiences, some universal truths emerged, even though we came from different angles.

- We are here to learn how to love ourselves and others unconditionally.
- Part of learning to love is about unconditionally forgiving ourselves and others.
- There is no judgment other than self-judgment on the other side, so why does anyone judge themselves or others here?
- We must look upon others with compassion, as we have no idea what scars they are concealing.
- Today is all we have.
- Finally, what we call love here is incomparable to what we both experienced on the other side. It is an all-enveloping warmth and safety that is difficult to describe. In short, it is all about love.

As I write this, I think about all the medical staff I have worked with in the past few months, and what they do comes down to love, too. All of the education and training they have is because they love others and want to help.

Am I afraid to die? Not in the least. Do I want to die when I know how wonderful it is? The answer to that is no. I have so much left to learn and enjoy here first.

I love you all. Thanks again for sharing my journey.

How does one describe the love that exists on the other side of a thin veil? You have read some of my experiences with it in this book, and may have read much more about it in my previous book, Do You Hear My Voice. *Almost everyone who has a near-death experience makes similar statements. You hear words like "complete," "overwhelming," and "perfect" as given descriptions.*

For me, it feels warm. When I encountered it, I felt safe and complete. Oh, how I wish I could package it and share it. Nothing compares.

Having experienced that, I sometimes get frustrated seeing how much hate and division exist now on this planet. Love strengthens, and hate only divides.

39

Infusion Day #9 – What is Loneliness?

AUGUST 1, 2023

I am now 75% done with the chemo. Yay, I can't wait for it to be finished. I made my last appointment today. Hopefully, on September 14th, I can ring the bell just outside the room where I sit.

What I am about to write, I do not write for sympathy or as a plea for help, but as a way to be as raw and vulnerable as possible. I had a dream last night that got me thinking. We pass through the birth canal alone, and later, we move back to the other side of the veil alone. Although loved ones meet us immediately after each move, the actual act of relocation in either direction, so to speak, is something we need to do alone.

The question remains: What do we do when we experience times of loneliness in between relocations?

In the past few months, I have gone from having my family together in May to being alone in June. I have two very independent children who have reached a point where they are beginning to experience adult lives and following their own paths. One is in the Bay Area beginning her life as a new teacher, and the other has moved to Hawaii to live, work, and be with the person she loves. I can't tell you how proud I am of them both.

My house is suddenly very quiet. I sometimes hear phantom noises, and it feels like one of the kids has walked through the door, but I know that is not true. I am there alone. Don't get me wrong; there are benefits to being alone. I can do whatever I want, on my schedule.

However, there are times when I feel a profound emptiness that penetrates deep into my emotions. And the question is, how do I deal with that? I know there is something to be learned, but what? My dream this morning pointed to something within the loneliness that I must learn from. So this time, I must dive into it instead of running from that feeling, and see what I can discover.

Wish me luck!

So, what can be found in loneliness? What did I learn? I discovered myself, and I love him. I know that might seem crazy, but I think one challenge that many of us face is learning to love and accept ourselves completely for just who we are, not what we have accomplished or those we associate with.

We must truly love ourselves as we are, at all times. There is something liberating in that acceptance. What a wonderful gift I found within the lesson of loneliness.

40

"Good to See No Sign of Cancer"

AUGUST 5, 2023

Yesterday, I had a CT scan to determine my treatment progress. This morning, I got a note from my oncologist telling me there are no signs of cancer. That is the best possible news I could receive. With three infusions left, I am exactly where I need to be.

With that comes an immense amount of gratitude – not only for the treatment's effectiveness but also for the dedication of the medical teams that have used their skills and knowledge to help me heal.

When I speak of medical teams, I think not only of the traditional ones but also of the spiritual assistance from which I have benefited. I also want to thank all of you who have sent me good vibes and prayers along the journey. It means a lot and has made a difference.

I still have a way to go, but I think I am in a good place now.

I honestly believe that there have been multiple important factors in my recovery. It felt like an interdisciplinary operation all around, each part working in harmony with the others. Had I not had the quick response from the extremely knowledgeable and trained medical staff, my cancer may have spread. Working on energetic causes of the tumor also aided the healing process tremendously, as I reached some core issues which may have contributed to the cancer.

However, without the love, support, and prayers from both sides of the veil, I am not sure that the medical and energetic treatments would have been as effective. The way I perceive it, I had the best medical and energetic healers diligently working on my behalf, all within a highly charged container of love and support. Take away any one of those factors and it wouldn't have worked nearly as well.

As I look back on all of this, I can never discount just how fortunate I have been.

41

It's a Miracle!

AUGUST 13, 2023

I spent today at an event called The Spirit Summit, mainly promoting my current and future books. It was a great experience. I met many lovely people, some of whom had read my first book and some who had never heard of it.

I loved talking to so many people; it is incredible how many have cancer stories. If it hasn't touched them personally, it has affected someone close to them. In some ways, when I hear stories of those who have had a rougher path, I felt pangs of "survivor's guilt." Why has my path been so much easier than others?

On my drive home, I played a game called "song roulette," where I listened to every third song. Today, the music that had the most impact was Queen's "The Miracle." I began to think of all the assistance and healing I have felt from so many of you, and was reminded of just how miraculous my path has been.

I just felt so lucky to be here on Earth at this time. I feel so fortunate to be the recipient of life's miracles, and I will never take it for granted.

I have often wondered what constitutes a miracle. Could it be attending a meditation retreat and learning methods of pain control a week before I even knew that I would need it? Or a doctor who had scheduled to go skiing with his family but canceled because of an ice storm, and suddenly became available to perform an emergency procedure on me which prevented further damage?

Or could it even be developing the cancer itself, opening me up to learning more about what is truly important in life?

Did I just say that?

Cancer has been a miracle for me. I completely believe that getting this disease has opened me up to many aspects of life that I was missing, and taught me so many beautiful lessons. Without it I would have missed some amazing insights that have been truly life changing.

42

Infusion Day #10 – This is It!

AUGUST 15, 2023

Only two more infusions left after this week. I am definitely in the home stretch.

On the way to the hospital today, my random song was an oldie but a goodie: "This is It," by Kenny Loggins. What a perfect song for the way I feel. In the lyrics, he sings that we decide how things go, there is no more waiting, and no one knows what the future may have in store for us.

It goes back to the idea that if we can make the best decisions based on the information we have at the time, that is all that is expected of us. If we make a mistake, we must ask for forgiveness, learn from it, and move on. It is all about learning while we are on this planet.

The most significant thing we need to learn is self-love, and the willingness to forgive ourselves for making the best choices we could at the time, even if they did not turn out the way we expected. In reality there should be nothing to regret, as each decision and action we take is about learning and growth.

That may sound simple, but I know that it is not. But there is so much personal evolution when we can see life through this lens.

As always, thank you for your love and support. It really makes a difference.

One interesting aspect of this is that forgiveness happens in our hearts. We do not need to wait for an apology or act of contrition from the one who may have wronged us. I had to learn to release it from within my heart. This is not always easy, but the more I practice it, the simpler it becomes.

43

I Don't Need Any Help! (Maybe I Do!)

AUGUST 26, 2023

Sometimes, becoming an empty nester comes with the desire to downsize. That is the position I was in this past week. In my mind, I had movers coming and they would do the bulk of the work. I just had to do the "little stuff." I had no idea that the little stuff would turn into many things. How so many little treasures (junk) can be hidden in one place is impressive.

Downsizing a home that once housed four to a place that would accommodate one caused me to create thirty large bags of "treasures." On the last day, I was extremely tired. The cumulative effect of the chemo combined with the sheer amount of manual labor in one week had exhausted me beyond where I should have been.

As I picked up one of the last bags, I twisted as I was lifting and felt a sudden "pop." It felt like a knife was jabbed in my lower back. With every step, I felt that stabbing pain. I knew I should be done, but I had committed to completing everything by that evening, so I worked through the pain.

As I was finishing, I kept thinking of the offers of help I'd received, but had been too proud to accept.

The next day when I woke, I attempted to stand but collapsed in bed after the pain shot from my lower back. I have spent the last couple of days mostly in bed.

What did I learn?

- I am not 20 anymore.
- It is okay to accept help from friends.
- I must listen to and respect my body.
- Despite the chemo and the pain, I did it! Is this part of my comeback?

I am still learning that it is okay to ask for help. It is part of my journey to learn vulnerability.

44

Infusion Day #11 – Almost Done

AUGUST 29, 2023

The woman next to me today finally finished her scheduled chemo sessions. When she left, she was escorted up front, where she rang the bell. I don't know this woman, but I somehow felt so proud of her and for what she has been through.

Anyone who has ever been through this experience knows that every day is a battle. Just getting to the bell ringing is such an accomplishment, and I have gained a greater appreciation for it. Just two weeks and two days from today, I will experience this moment of achievement.

Each day, I gain a greater appreciation for this thing we call life. I am so lucky to be here currently and to have had my experiences with my cancer. It has allowed me to see so much beauty and to find a sense of gratitude that had previously been invisible to me.

Earlier, I shared a quote from *Good Will Hunting* that fits so well for this experience:

> "You will have bad times, but that'll always wake you up to the good stuff you weren't paying attention to."
> – Robin Williams as Sean Maguire in *Good Will Hunting*

Can someone love cancer? Is it possible to love the hardships in life?

I remember some of the most difficult and challenging courses and teachers I had while I was going to school. They were always the most demanding, but I learned the most about the subject and about my ability to succeed despite the obstacles.

As much as I hate to say it, the difficulties make learning so much more profound.

45

Reframing the Day

SEPTEMBER 2, 2023

Today I attended a football game. It was the 10th-ranked University of Washington against my alma mater, Boise State University. Since it was the season's first game, one hoped it would start with a win for the ol' home school. Today didn't turn out that way.

I had invited a former coworker, a UW alum who now lives in Ventura, CA, to join me for the game. Seeing him again and catching up was great, but as the game progressed, I knew this was not my day – quite the opposite, in fact. My team ended up losing by a substantial margin.

During the game, I began to think back on all I had learned on my recent journey. I looked around the beautiful stadium where I was sitting and saw the boats on Lake Washington, and the clear skies and sunshine all around me. At that moment, even though my team was losing, I felt so fortunate to be there.

After the game, my friend and I walked about a mile to get some dinner at the closest restaurant to the stadium. Once again, the toll the cancer treatment had taken on my body became apparent several times as we stopped to rest.

While we enjoyed our meal, we began discussing childhood trauma and its effects on adults. We both talked about our experiences with trauma and trauma therapy. Comparing notes was very helpful. We promised to continue the conversation, and I left feeling a deeper connection to my friend.

Ultimately, today turned into a great day despite the loss, but when is time spent with a good friend ever a loss?

What a gift it has been to have the ability to define or place meaning on a set of circumstances. I really could have looked at that situation and been upset with the game loss, and the health struggle of walking a mile to our destination.

Instead, I found myself looking for the beauty of where I was, the compassion of a friend, and a deep conversation about life. What an amazing day that really was, and what value to be able to see it that way.

46

Mini Epiphany

SEPTEMBER 6, 2023

This morning before work, I was scrolling on a social media platform, and I read a post from an old friend. I found myself disagreeing with almost everything I read. Then something clicked and I asked myself, "Do I still love this person despite this post?"

My answer was, "Yes!"

Then I asked myself other questions. "Can I still love someone regardless of their actions? Is there a form of love that supersedes any action someone could take? Is it possible to not approve of a person's actions and still love them?"

My answer to all the questions was the same: "Yes!"

I believe true love is the greatest force in the Universe. I love you all, and thank you for joining me on this fantastic journey.

I have often heard the phrase, "Love the person, hate the sin." While there was no sin here other than a differing opinion, can we learn to separate out a person's actions and rhetoric from their identity as a human and a spiritual being?

Is it possible to just accept others for all their differences, without judgment? Imagine where our society would be if we could all do this. Do you remember my conversation with my friend who'd had a near-death experience? One of our conclusions was that there is no judgment, other than a self-evaluation of our lives, on the other side of the veil – so why do we judge others here?

It is so easy to point a finger, but so much more difficult to love others when we may disagree with them. It is okay to have different opinions and to fight for what you believe is right, but so important to also never stop loving

47

We All Want to Leave a Positive Impact on Others

SEPTEMBER 8, 2023

Next week, I will finish my chemo treatments, and I am still cancer-free. Over the next few days, I will wrap up this online journal and summarize some of my learnings.

CaringBridge has been an absolute blessing to me. It has enabled me to share what I have learned and get feedback from many of you. Your encouragement during good and bad times has really kept me going.

Throughout this journey, I have been humbled by the number of private messages I have received from many telling me that because I have been so open with my journey, they have gone in for their first colonoscopy. I just received another today, so it is front of mind. If that is my only impact on the world, I have succeeded.

However, I hope that some of my other experiences have benefited you. I am truly so grateful to have walked down this path.

You will have to forgive some of the redundancies, but over the next week, I will take time to highlight what I have learned, and what has impacted me the most.

48

Infusion Day #12 – Last One

SEPTEMBER 12, 2023

There is so much going on in my head today. I am thrilled that I will be done this week and can finally ring the bell. Six months of this routine has been a blessing but also a challenge, and a journey where I have learned so much about life and what makes me tick.

It has also shown me different ways I can serve others who may have to walk down the same road in the future.

After today, I will have the slow drip chemo for two days. On Thursday, I will be unplugged for the last time. There is a sense of freedom, knowing I will now be able to move into the next phase of my life. I must admit that I have become comfortable with this routine, but I'm also happy to leave it in the past.

Later I will be posting several summary posts on topics I believe are critical, each of which deserves its own focus.

49

What I Learned about Gratitude

SEPTEMBER 12, 2023

You have seen me post numerous times about my gratitude throughout this process. That has to be one of the greatest blessings I have experienced from the time I was diagnosed until now.

I feel so grateful for the outpouring of love, positive vibes, and prayers that have come my way, both professionally and personally.

I'm grateful that I work for a company that has provided me with great health benefits, and that I have a fantastic boss who has given me the space to take those extra hours off when I hit the chemo wall, as I call it. I can't express just how important that is.

I am incredibly grateful for all the beautiful comments I've received on these journal entries. Between those and the private messages I have received on the side, I always took strength from your optimism.

Sometimes, the message to keep going has come from a surprising source. I have had positive comments from business associates I only worked with for a limited time, and friends I have not seen in person for over thirty years. Each one gives me strength and helps me to carry on. I am so thankful for all those who have supported me along the way, including those who have virtually walked with me.

In addition, I have sometimes felt gratitude for the sunlight streaming through my window in the morning, especially when I realize that I get to live and experience another day. Some days have been challenging, but I have learned to appreciate them even more as they help me realize how fortunate I am for the good days.

This is a fantastic world, and even though we have challenges, we are so lucky to be here now.

As I quoted in my first post, taken from my book *Do You Hear My Voice? Discovering Jessica Again*:

> "Enjoy the ride! I am talking about every beautiful thing and action that you see, and the adversities you face. Being human is such a remarkable thing. One day, you will look back on it all and begin to comprehend the magnificence in all that you experience and how fortunate you have been.
>
> "Each soul has had hundreds of lives in which they have the opportunity to learn. You are so blessed to have this opportunity. I know that it may be difficult to understand

from the human side, but each experience you have on Earth is a blessing. Each morning, you should wake with a thankful heart for the opportunity that you have to be there. Do not waste days living in fear, for fear will destroy you."

– Jessica

So much has been written about gratitude, and rightfully so. I do not really know what it is about having cancer that kicks the intensity of gratitude into high gear, but it is a thing and something that has been expressed by many who have been diagnosed with this disease.

Maybe the greater understanding of the finiteness of this life, or the many acts of kindness one receives, causes the appreciation to increase. I know one day, I found myself watching a bee flying from flower to flower as it collected pollen. The beauty of this simple act touched my heart, and I felt so thankful that I had the opportunity to witness it. People who know me well may tell you I do not typically do that.

Occasionally, I found myself looking for more ways to grow that feeling. They were not difficult to find. Sometimes, what made me the happiest occurred on the most difficult of days. Do you have any idea how great it was to find an extra tube of toothpaste on a day when I thought I was out and didn't have the energy to go to the store?

In today's society we may have trained ourselves to only look for things to fear, and not what we can be grateful for. However, if you begin actively looking for things to be grateful for, it will change your life in the most profound ways.

50

What I Learned about Anger and Forgiveness

SEPTEMBER 12, 2023

When I looked at my cancer, I realized there was not just one factor that caused the formation of my tumor. I had issues with diet, exercise, and pent-up anger. That anger was not directed outward but toward myself, often for not being good enough. The first two are relatively easy lifestyle changes, but I found the third to be the most challenging.

I knew the amount of stored-up anger I held onto had to be released, but how? I ended up working with a fantastic bio-energy healer, Molly Grove, who helped me release the long-held anger through a series of bio-energy healing sessions and emotional work, which took a deep dive into the origins of my rage.

Still, I had to learn how to not recreate that anger toward myself or others. I had to break that internal pattern. How did I do that? Above all else, I am learning to forgive myself and others.

We are all on this Earth trying to make the best decisions we can based on the best information we have at the time. Suppose some of those choices have adverse consequences. In that case, I am learning to realize those decisions were made with the best available information at the time. I am learning to not only forgive myself but to forgive others for similar choices.

Some may think it impossible to forgive yourself and others for past indiscretions. I can tell you that releasing the initial rage and learning to forgive will ultimately change your life. I credit my healing just as much to this as to the chemotherapy.

Please don't let your internal fury harm your health. Learn to release your anger and learn to forgive for the benefit of your mental, emotional, and physical wellbeing.

I recently spoke to a professional counselor friend, and I was telling him about this book. When I told him that one of the themes of this book is forgiveness, he squirmed a bit and asked if I really understood just how difficult that can be. I told him that I did, but what are the consequences of not doing it?

I agree that some of the issues many deal with will not go away easily, but just because it may be difficult and take years, it doesn't make the effort any less important to one's overall health and wellbeing. Have I forgiven everyone and everything I should? The answer is no, but I do see energetic changes when I finally let some of the big things go. Freedom can definitely be found on the other side.

Sometimes, the most courageous action you can take is to forgive. It is much easier to hold on to the anger or the grudge. Focusing those emotions on an event or person is perceived as less painful than actually dealing with or releasing them. But real courage happens when we learn to face and heal those things, and consciously decide to not let that event or person control us forever.

What I did learn through this process is that no matter how I buried those emotions they continued to intensify, even if I was not fully aware. It wasn't until I looked at them in the light of day and made the decision to release those things that I became so much freer.

If you could change anything in your past, would you? I heard Martha Beck ask that in a podcast once. Most of us can create a laundry list of regrets, but would changing those fundamentally change the person you have become? Who we are now is a compilation of every decision and action we have taken at any given time. Take one away, and it could change everything about who we are or where we are in life.

Take the cancer away from my life, and every decision that led up to it, and I would not have had the insights about life and love that I have been blessed with.

51

What I Learned about Love

SEPTEMBER 12, 2023

The outpouring of love I have felt worldwide underlies everything on this journey. These days, our society focuses so much on creating fear and hate that I can only imagine what the world would look like if the same energy were concentrated on learning to love, instead of demonizing what is not understood.

Despite all the focus on fear, I am still convinced that love, in its purest form, is the most potent force in the Universe. It has been the expressions of love flowing toward me that have made all the difference on this path. These expressions have been directed through the good vibes and prayers many of you sent me. They have also come through text messages or comments on this journal; each time someone writes to me, I can feel the love behind the effort.

I was reminded recently in a dream that one of the main reasons we come to Earth is to learn how to love through hardships. This journey I have been on over the last nine months is a perfect example. I have learned many lessons, including experiencing love through severe challenges.

Remember, we are all a piece of this thing called love, which is core to who we are. If we could only remember and develop that, the world would be so much better.

I believe love can be a complex word. I firmly believe we are all inherently love. Love is the energy that not only powers us but also the Universe. We come to this planet as infants and forget everything, and our challenge is to work through all the difficulties in life to learn new and different aspects of the energy of love. Throughout my journey over the last few years, I have had the opportunity to experience a small but powerful fraction of this universal energy. When I came in contact with it, it felt overwhelming while also being perfectly comforting.

Sometimes, I believe the ability to express love, whether verbally or through action, may come so naturally to some that they may not consciously understand what they're doing. To others, it comes from a lifetime of service, in which the repetition becomes a habit. Their actions may be new to others, and they feel a high from expressing it.

It is the expressions of that love that I have felt the most during this journey. Teaching others to meditate expresses love. And who can deny that a boss willing to walk a few miles on an employee's behalf, and give that same employee time to recover when needed, demonstrates love? Weren't those who virtually walked with me, prayed for me, or sent good vibes showing love too? What about the medical professionals who trained for years to be of service to someone like me – isn't that a demonstration of love? Wouldn't you say that a singer sharing their soul through music demonstrates love?

And what about a mother volunteering to bring me into this lifetime in order to help me understand love more completely, and then demonstrating that love over and over again even from across the veil?

I had one friend whom I had known since elementary school; even though we lost touch with each other for a while, he took the time to knit me a cashmere cap when he found out about my illness. This is just one more example of expressing love.

You do not have to have cancer to experience this in your life. Just look around. Expressions of love are everywhere. Sometimes we don't classify them as such, or consciously realize what they are, but they are there. Start tuning into the good around you.

As it says in my previous book, "Do not waste days living in fear, for fear will destroy you." The energy of love is the opposite of fear, and a most powerful force.

52

Second Chances

SEPTEMBER 13, 2023

When I was thinking about all the blessings from my cancer diagnosis up until now, I missed a big one. I now have a second chance, at everything. Had I not had urgent surgery to place a stent in my bowel, performed by a doctor who had planned to go skiing but couldn't due to icy December roads, I probably would not be here to type this today. Had I not had a skilled doctor remove the tumor when he did, I might not be in the same good place I am today.

Had I not worked with a talented and gifted healer to help me deal with my anger, I would not be as optimistic as I am today. Had I not gone to the Infusion Center for the last six months, I would not feel as confident about my current situation as I do now. And had I not received the support and love from all of you, I am not sure what my mental and emotional condition would be.

I now have a second chance with my life. The question is, what do I do with that? The first thing that comes to mind is that I have had poisons dumped into my body for the last six months. I must devote time and effort to healing my body from that. So, I will be devoting more time to my health and recovery.

But how do I pass it forward when blessed with so much? I have some ideas, but you must wait and see with that part.

I would challenge you: You don't need to be in the same situation I was in to create change in the world. If we all look at our lives as blessings, it becomes easier to share them with others. Just imagine what we could do if we all shared the love that is in our hearts with others, and they, in turn, passed it on to even more people. Could we not make the world a better place?

Please use my second chance as an excuse to help others through your continued sharing of love and healing energy, as you did for me – the ripple effect can be enormous.

53

What Can I Learn Today?

SEPTEMBER 13, 2023

In my summary journal entries, I wrote about gratitude, releasing anger, forgiving, and love. Still, I forgot another important lesson I learned.

Every morning, I ask, "What can I learn today?"

Framing the day that way has changed how I look at my life, and has gotten me through some difficult times. If something good happens, I ask that question. If I am facing difficulty, I ask that question. I am telling you, taking that one simple step each morning and then reviewing the day before you sleep will change your life. It has changed me.

I wish you all the best as you go out and face your challenges, whatever they may be. And remember, it is not taking the easy path where we learn the most; it is the one that takes us beyond the mountains.

I love you and wish you the best on your journey through life

54

Yesterday, I Rang the Bell. Today, I am Just Tired

SEPTEMBER 15, 2023

It is not the act of ringing the bell that tired me, but the last chemical cocktail injected into my veins this week that I didn't consider in advance. So, today has been a recovery day. The rebuilding begins next week. I am glad the chemo phase is over, and I look forward to bigger and better things. In the words of Buzz Lightyear, "To infinity and beyond!"

I am so thankful for everyone who joined me yesterday, both physically and virtually; I could really feel everyone's presence.

Ringing the bell seemed to be such a momentous occasion, but while I looked at it as an ending, it became a beginning to experience a new life full of new and different challenges. Sometimes, more mountains exist beyond the mountains, but the tools developed and muscles strengthened in traversing the first set of mountains can only benefit someone as they climb new ones.

55

Afterword

When I finished my online journal, I thought my journey was ending. I had completed the treatment; I was done. Little did I know that the physical recovery would take quite a bit of time; I was very weak for nearly three months following chemo. Traveling for work, something that I usually love, challenged me. I felt devastated and at times, I wondered if I could continue. Over time and with care for my body, my health slowly began to return, and today, I am nearly back to pre-cancer levels.

Mentally and emotionally, it has been such an interesting adventure – one I certainly did not anticipate. What I learned on my path changed the way I look at this thing called life and the obstacles in my way. I have often wondered how different our lives would be if, instead of cursing the challenges, we could learn to embrace them and love them for how they allow us to learn and grow.

Some of the key points I learned on this journey are below.

- Being grateful for even the smallest things can change your focus in life.
- Holding on to anger and fear can be detrimental to your health.
- Forgiveness of yourself and others is a powerful treatment.
- Love is the greatest power in the world and can help you overcome your fears.
- Each day, I ask, "What can I learn today?"

Of those, I have felt more love than I could have possibly imagined. The way I interpret it, it is the purest love at its highest level of expression. I not only felt it from those on Earth, but I believe I also had an incredible amount of love flowing from the other side of the veil.

That immense love pulled me through this experience. As I mentioned earlier, I wish I could just bottle it up and share it with each of my readers.

I am so grateful for my second chance, whether it is for one day or thousands of days. I hope you can gain courage from something you may have read here. I wish you the best on your journey through this amazing thing called life.

For more information or to donate to CaringBridge, please visit: https://www.caringbridge.com.

If you are interested in learning more about bio-energy healing, please visit Molly's website: https://mollygrove.com.

If you are interested in learning more about past lives, soul lessons, and karmic relationship connections, please visit my editor Vanessa's website: https://highpriestessinchucks.com.

You can learn more about dream interpretation and find April at the Aisling Dream Interpretation website: https://www.dream-analysis.com.

Please feel free to contact me at bruce@bruceklein.me with any questions or comments. I am currently working on some resources to assist those who may be facing these kinds of challenges.

If you want to stay updated on my other projects, please visit https://bruceklein.me or follow me on Facebook and Instagram at "BruceKleinAuthor."

Bruce Klein, a native of the Pacific Northwest, is a proud father of two remarkable daughters. His professional career has been primarily centered on corporate international trade compliance. However, his earlier years were enriched by more than seven years in Asia, where he worked in education. This experience cultivated a deep respect for the continent's diverse beliefs. Raised in a strict religious environment, Bruce chose to distance himself from all spiritual pursuits in his twenties. Yet, in 2017, an unexpected spiritual renaissance reshaped his life in unforeseen ways.

In his first book, "Do You Hear My Voice? Discovering Jessica Again," published in 2021, Bruce recounts his personal spiritual awakening. It narrates his journey from a conservative religious background to a later realization that love is the greatest force on earth.

www.ingramcontent.com/pod-product-compliance
Lightning Source LLC
Chambersburg PA
CBHW060609080526
44585CB00013B/748